NATIONAL GEOGRAPHIC

Stories From the
UNDERGROUND
RAILROAD

PATHFINDER EDITION

By Peter Winkler

CONTENTS

Eyewitness on the
UNDERGROUND
RAILROAD

History owes a lot to William Still.
He helped hundreds of runaway slaves.
And he recorded their amazing stories.

BY PETER WINKLER

Still

Meet William Still. He's someone to remember next time you wonder if one person can make a difference.

Still was born on a New Jersey farm in 1821. His parents were former slaves. In 1841, at age 20, Still moved to Philadelphia. In 1847 he got a job at the Pennsylvania Anti-Slavery Society.

Within a few years, Still was a key member of the **Underground Railroad.** As you probably know, the "railroad" had no trains. It was a web of people—black and white—who helped runaway slaves head north. **Fugitives,** or runaways, often tried to reach Canada, which had outlawed slavery.

Working on the Underground Railroad meant breaking the law. So Still had to balance courage and caution. He did it well. Before the Civil War began in 1861, Still helped about 800 fugitives. Sixty or so were children.

Still gave money, food, and clothing to runaways. He found them places to stay, sometimes in his own home. Then Still pointed the former slaves toward other "stations," or safe places, on the Underground Railroad.

Still did something else too. He listened. Fugitives told him about their lives and their escapes. Still kept careful notes of everything he learned. By doing so, he created what experts call an **oral history.** That's a record of people's *memories* and stories.

Those notes grew into a thick book called *The Underground Rail Road*. Published in 1872, it is an important resource for studying African-American history. The three stories that follow are adapted from Still's work. They show the courage and creativity that helped some slaves escape to freedom.

WILLIAM AND ELLEN CRAFT

Slaves rarely escaped from the southernmost states. Canada was just too far away. Hunger, exhaustion, or slave hunters defeated most runaways. But William and Ellen Craft found a daring way to leave Georgia—in disguise.

Ellen's skin was pale, almost white. So she dressed up like a young white man in poor health. "He" would ride the train to see doctors up north. William would go along, pretending to be a faithful servant.

The Crafts disguised Ellen carefully. She cut her hair and put on male clothes. She wore dark glasses and bandages. And she put her right arm in a sling. That way no one knew she couldn't write.

The trip went perfectly. No one guessed the Crafts' secret. Over the years, the Crafts had earned money by doing extra work. So they stayed in fine hotels all along the way. They reached Philadelphia safely. Then off came the glasses, the bandages, and the man's clothing. Still wrote that he could never forget "the impression made by their arrival."

After a rest in Philadelphia, the Crafts moved to Boston. They spent two years there. Then they learned that their old master had hired slave hunters to kidnap them. So they fled to England and lived there happily for the next 20 years.

Badge worn by freed slaves in Charleston, South Carolina

Wordwise

fugitive: runaway

oral history: eyewitness stories and memories told to an interviewer

ordeal: harsh experience

Underground Railroad: informal web of people who helped slaves escape

HENRY "BOX" BROWN

Henry Brown was a slave in Richmond, Virginia. He was also, William Still wrote, "a man of invention." Brown thought about running away on foot. But slave hunters would probably catch him. So he tried something completely different.

Brown got a carpenter to make a wooden crate. It was three feet long and two feet wide. And it stood two and a half feet high. Brown lined the box with cloth. After all, the crate would hold important cargo—himself.

Could Brown survive such a strange, hard trip? He wanted to try. To get air, he drilled small holes into the sides of the box. He put a container of water and some biscuits into the crate. Then he climbed in.

A friend nailed the box shut. He shipped it to Philadelphia, where the Underground Railroad was active. An express train carried the crate—and Brown—to Pennsylvania. The whole trip took 26 hours.

William Still and several others opened the amazing package. "The witnesses," Still said, "will never forget that moment. Rising up in his box, [Brown] reached out his hand, saying, 'How do you do, gentlemen?'"

Brown spent several days with Still and other Underground Railroad workers in Philadelphia. They nicknamed him Henry "Box" Brown. Brown then headed to Boston, Massachusetts, and became a popular antislavery speaker.

"THE MEMORABLE TWENTY-EIGHT"

Aaron Cornish hoped to be set free when his master died. That's what the old man had promised, after all. But the master never put his pledge in writing. So Cornish wound up with a harsh new owner.

It was time to escape. Cornish and his wife, Daffney, decided to flee their home in Cambridge, Maryland. So did many of their friends. All together the group had 28 people. There were 17 adults and 11 children.

They set out on a stormy night. Rain pounded the fugitives. But it also made it harder for slave hunters and their bloodhounds to find anyone.

The storm lasted three days. Several children got sick. And everyone got hungry. Their only food was dried corn and some crackers. "It is impossible," wrote Still, "to imagine the **ordeal** they were passing." But everyone kept walking.

"It was exceedingly agreeable," Still said, "to hear even the little children testify that in the most trying hour on the road, not for a moment did they want to go back."

Step after soggy step led the fugitives to Philadelphia. "The memorable Twenty-Eight," as Still called them, were "in tattered garments, hungry, sick, and penniless."

In Philadelphia, Still recorded, the runaways "were kindly clothed, fed, doctored, and sent on their way rejoicing."

Rag doll from the Civil War era

ASK. LISTEN. WRITE.

William Still created an oral history of the Underground Railroad. An oral history is a collection of stories, memories, and related facts told to an interviewer. Most slaves could not read or write. So they told their stories to Still, who then wrote them down.

You can create an oral history of your community. Start by talking to a relative, friend, or neighbor who has lived there for a while. To get the person talking, you will need to write down some questions.

Oral History Tips

- **Phrase questions so that the answer is more than just "yes" or "no."**

- **Start some questions with the five W's: Who? What? Where? When? Why?**

- **Involve the person's senses. For instance, what sounds or smells does the person remember?**

- **Encourage the person to give examples of how things have changed.**

- **Toward the end of the conversation, ask if there was anything you should have asked but didn't. This can lead to interesting stories.**

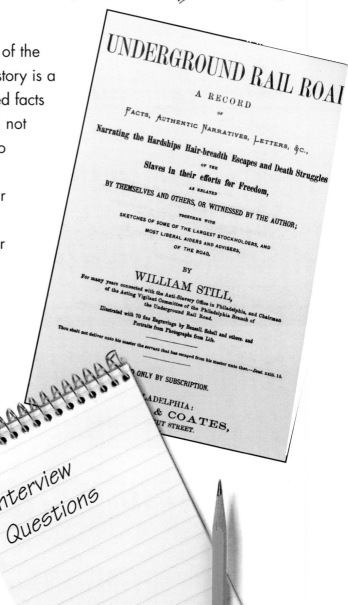

UNDERGROUND RAIL ROAD

A RECORD

OF

FACTS, AUTHENTIC NARRATIVES, LETTERS, &c.,

Narrating the Hardships Hair-breadth Escapes and Death Struggles

OF THE

Slaves in their efforts for Freedom,

AS RELATED

BY THEMSELVES AND OTHERS, OR WITNESSED BY THE AUTHOR;

TOGETHER WITH

SKETCHES OF SOME OF THE LARGEST STOCKHOLDERS, AND

MOST LIBERAL AIDERS AND ADVISERS,

OF THE ROAD.

BY

WILLIAM STILL,

For many years connected with the Anti-Slavery Office in Philadelphia, and Chairman of the Acting Vigilant Committee of the Philadelphia Branch of the Underground Rail Road.

Illustrated with 70 fine Engravings by Bensell, Schell and others, and Portraits from Photographs from Life.

Thou shalt not deliver unto his master the servant that has escaped from his master unto thee.—*Deut. xxiii. 15.*

ONLY BY SUBSCRIPTION.

ADELPHIA:

& COATES,

UT STREET.

Interview Questions

This notice offers a reward for a runaway slave.

Journey

Slavery was legal in southern states. It was outlawed in northern states, Canada, and Mexico. So runaway slaves often traveled hundreds of miles to reach freedom.

Some slaves took southern routes. They traveled to Texas and then crossed into Mexico. Or they fled by boat from Florida.

Many others followed the Underground Railroad to northern states, where slavery was outlawed. Some even fled to Canada or across the Atlantic Ocean to England.

These journeys were long and risky. At any moment, runaways could be captured and sent back to slavery. That's because of a law that was passed in 1850. The law made escaping slavery harder than ever before.

Hunted North and South

The Fugitive Slave Act of 1850 meant that slaves were never free. It said that they had to be sent back to their owners. That was true even if they reached a "free" state. Many runaway slaves were captured and returned to slavery because of this law.

Of course, being captured didn't mean the slaves would stay. Harriet Jacobs, who wrote *Life of a Slave Girl*, escaped many times. She traveled for years, not weeks or months. Eventually, she found freedom.

The Fight for Freedom

For many years, slave states and free states battled over the issue of slavery. These conflicts led to the Civil War and freedom for all slaves. Even today, the stories from the Underground Railroad remind us of the value—and costs—of freedom.

This group of runaway slaves worked together to find freedom.

to Freedom

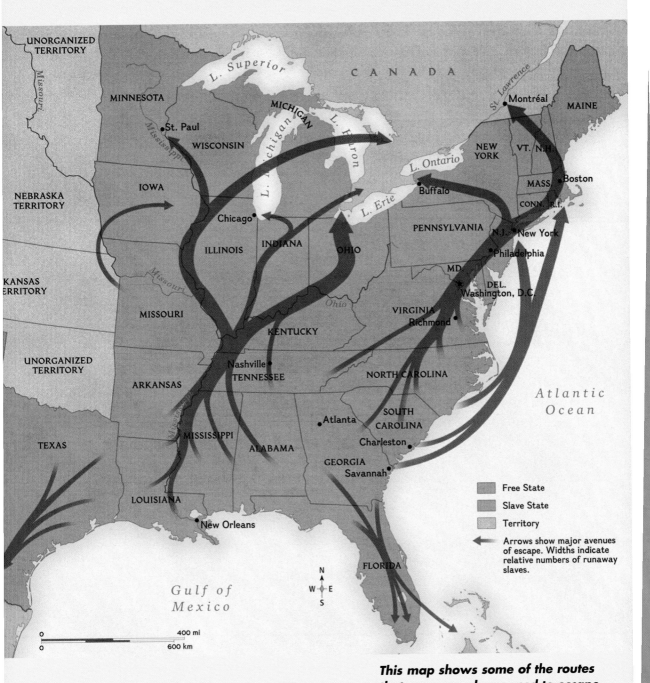

This map shows some of the routes that runaway slaves used to escape.

9

Underground Heroes

OHIO HISTORICAL SOCIETY (BOTH)

Rhoda Jones was a member of the Underground Railroad in Ohio.

unaway slaves faced great dangers when they escaped. So did the people who helped them. They risked prison and even death to help slaves reach freedom. In many cases, they gambled their safety for people they didn't even know—and would probably never see again. Who were these heroes of the Underground Railroad?

Working Against Slavery

Members of the Underground Railroad were ordinary men and women from every walk of life. Some were freed or escaped slaves. Some belonged to religious groups. Some were from the North. Others were from the slave-holding South.

The members of the Underground Railroad had different backgrounds. They had different reasons for helping runaway slaves on their journeys. Yet they all shared a common belief. They thought people should not have to live in slavery.

Risks of the Railroad

Helping slaves escape was dangerous work. According to the law, people could be punished for aiding a runaway slave. They might be fined or put in jail. The greatest danger, however, was from supporters of slavery. They sometimes injured or killed people who helped slaves escape.

Even so, many people accepted the risks. Take Rhoda Jones, for example. She lived in Ohio. Some people in that state had been killed for their work on the Underground Railroad. Still, Jones opened her home to runaway slaves.

The Gift of Freedom

Jones was just one of the thousands who risked great danger to help others. The members of the Underground Railroad didn't get money for their work. Most never became famous. Yet they were all willing to put their lives at risk to help others find freedom.

These twenty men were arrested for helping just one slave escape.

UNDERGROUND RAILROAD

**Answer these questions to find out
what you learned from the book.**

1 What was the Underground
Railroad?

2 Who was William Still? How did
he help people escape slavery?

3 Who worked on the
Underground Railroad?

4 Why was escaping slavery
difficult and dangerous?

5 How does Still's oral history
help people today learn
about slavery?